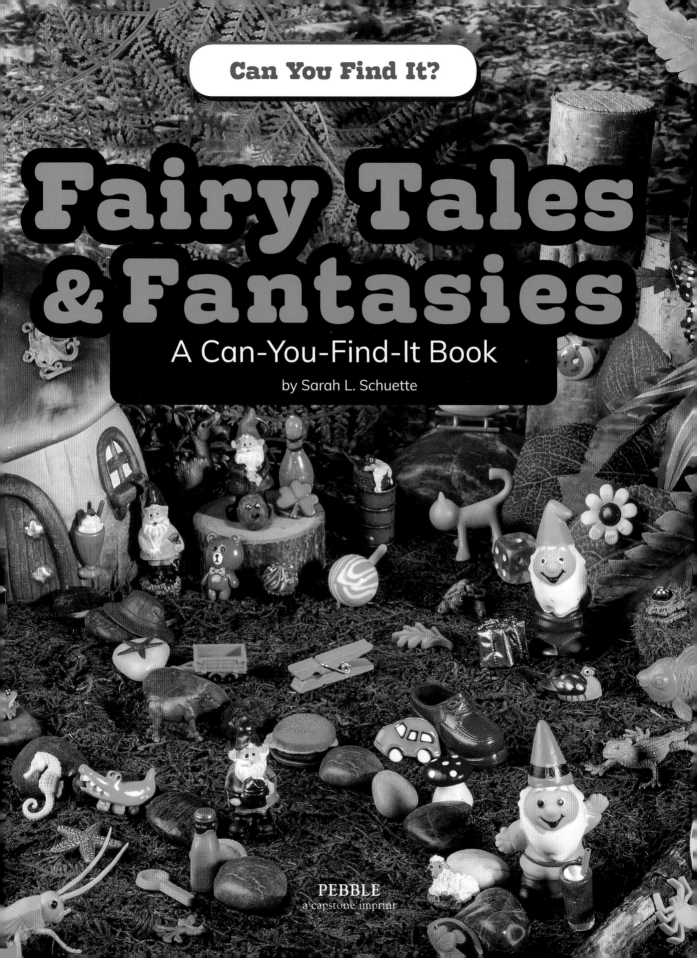

Can You Find It?

Fairy Tales
& Fantasies

A Can-You-Find-It Book

by Sarah L. Schuette

PEBBLE
a capstone imprint

Red Riding Hood

Can you find these things?

 moon

 butterfly

 guitar

 fish

 cupcake robot hamster  grasshopper lamp saw

Fairy Princess

Can you find these things?

strawberry

dragon

seahorse

unicorn

horseshoe

pumpkin

broom

hanger

spoon

shovel

Troll Bridge

Can you find
these things?

owl   violin   hamburger   lighthouse

camper

birdhouse

fawn

turkey

chicken

taxi

Dragon's Lair

Can you find
these things?

rose

bee

crown

pepper

 snail

 fox

 mushroom

 starfish

 trumpet

 frog

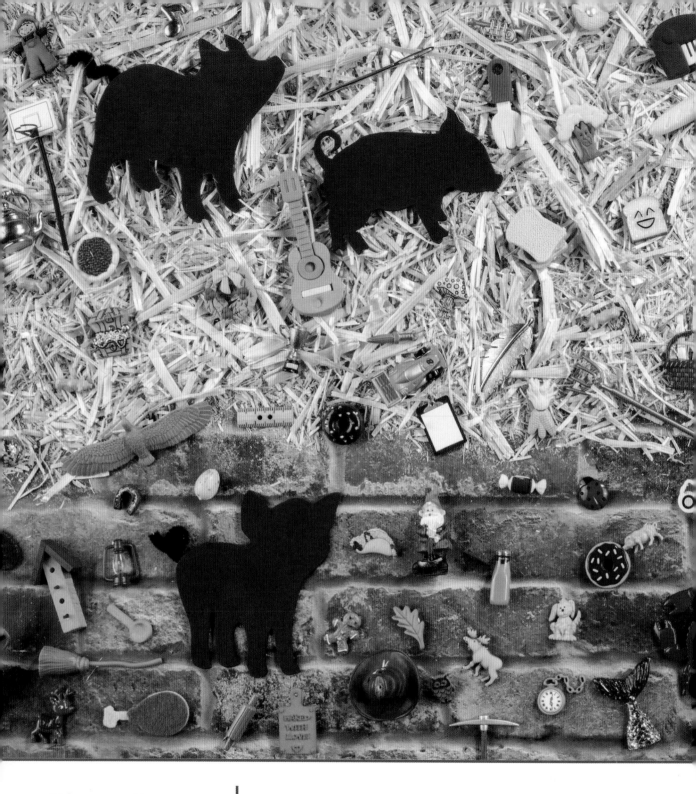

Three Pigs

Can you find
these things?

bacon

mouse

baseball
bat

wrench

 lantern

 moose

 needle

 ruler

 feather

 beaver

Mermaids

Can you find
these things?

carrot

Pegasus

dragon

bluebird

 sandwich  canoe flute cup swan pencil

Gnome Home

Can you find
these things?

spider

clover

dinosaur

duck

glass

hot
dog

hat

boot

acorn

lamb

Magical Rainbow

Can you find these things?

avocado

wagon

flipper

scooter

 tractor

 flashlight

 chicken

 goldfish

 tugboat

 hand

Frog Prince

Can you find these things?

 motorcycle

 scissors

 donkey

 magic lamp

bridge

fly

snake

hockey
skate

hammer

trophy

Jack's Beanstalk

Can you find these things?

tooth

blender

key

squirrel

 bin

 shirt

 sword

 pirate ship

 cactus

 robot

Fairy World

Can you find
these things?

turtle

shark

teddy
bear

tomato

gift

bananas

hair dryer

castle

bunny

grapes

Enchanted Forest

Can you find these things?

helicopter

heart

tent

basketball

sunglasses

rhino

spray
bottle

camel

Saturn

pear

Princess and the Pea

Can you find these things?

 Igloo

 koala

 elephant

 anchor

 sailboat umbrella dust pan whisk candle pea

Snow White

Can you find
these things?

pretzel

french
fries

ax

taco

Turn the page for the answer key!

skunk

toilet paper

bat

piano

spiderweb

bike

Psst! Did you know that Pebs the Pebble was hiding
in EVERY PUZZLE in this book?

It's true! Go back and look! Hi.

Look for other books in this series:

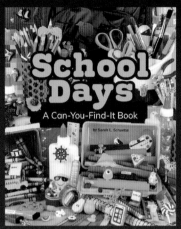
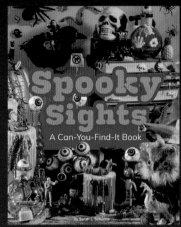

The author dedicates this book her friend, former homecoming queen,
Kitty Jo Collins, of Henderson, MN.

Pebble Sprout is published by Pebble, an imprint of Capstone.
1710 Roe Crest Drive, North Mankato, Minnesota 56003
www.capstonepub.com

Library of Congress Cataloging-in-Publication Data is available on the Library
of Congress website.
ISBN 978-1-9771-2257-5 (library binding)
ISBN 978-1-9771-2623-8 (paperback)
ISBN 978-1-9771-2309-1 (eBook PDF)

Summary: Show kids their favorite fairy tales and fantasies with this fun
seek-and-find title. Hundreds of objects are hidden inside full-color photo puzzles
of fairy-tale and fantasy characters, settings, and more. Each to-find list includes
pictographs and word labels to engage pre-readers and early readers alike.

Image Credits
All photos by Capstone Studio: Karon Dubke

Editorial Credits
Shelly Lyons, editor; Heidi Thompson, designer; Marcy Morin, set stylist;
Morgan Walters, media researcher; Kathy McColley, production specialist

Printed and bound in China.
3322